What Are You Feeling?

FEELINGS BOOKS FOR CHILDREN

Children's Emotions & Feelings Books

Let's Begin With types of feelings

Happy

Disappointed

cheeky

SaD

EXciteD

Angry

SCaReD

ConfuseD

Hurt

OPPOSITES

happy

sad

confident

scareD

Busy

lazy

Bored

excited

afraiD

Brave

angry

happy

together / in love

apart / heart-Broken

friendly

Bully

SiCK

healthy

kind

mean

furious

calm

Let's identify some emotions with these quizzes!

- [ ] confused

- [ ] happy

- [ ] angry

- [ ] afraid

- [ ] cheeky
- [ ] suspicious
- [ ] sad
- [ ] glad

- [ ] excited

- [ ] bored

- [ ] sleepy

- [ ] mean

- [ ] exhausted

- [ ] furious

- [ ] surprised

- [ ] thoughtful

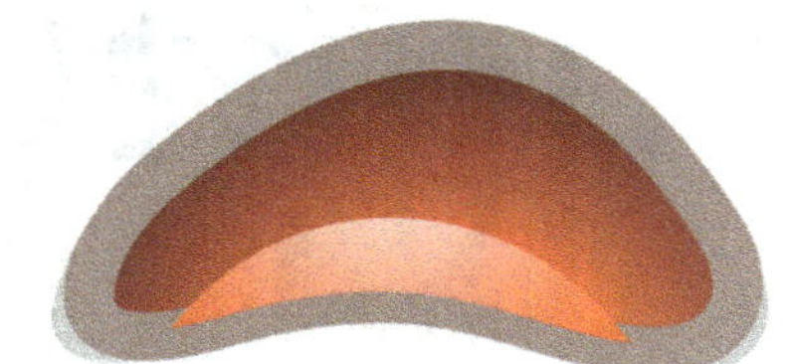

- [ ] happy
- [ ] calm
- [ ] friendly
- [ ] disappointed

- [ ] crying
- [ ] mad
- [ ] shocked
- [ ] pleased

answers

 happy

 furious

 sad

 disappointed

 excited

 shocked

Visit
BABY PROFESSOR
EDUCATION KIDS
www.BabyProfessorBooks.com
to download Free Baby Professor eBooks
and view our catalog of new and exciting
Children's Books